This is dedicated
to the person I was at seventeen years of age,
when I was eager to read a book like this
that could answer the questions that haunted me
when I was full of questions about life
and still deciding what I should do with my own,

and to everyone who is haunted by questions about
the meaning of life
and is still young at heart enough
and free and courageous enough
to be able to choose
what to do with it.

ISBN: 150528788X
ISBN 13: 9781505287882
Library of Congress Control Number: 2014921506
CreateSpace Independent Publishing Platform
North Charleston, South Carolina

a new dawn

Turn On the Lights and Turn Up the Love

Rodolfo León

Contents

A Note to the Reader

This book contains links to information and videos that support or clarify the ideas conveyed in the text. Please feel free to contact me to request an e-mail with these links so that you can more easily access these links by simply clicking on them. My name is Rodolfo but I go by David, and you can reach me at dleon19@atlanticbb.net (or at my backup e-mail address, which is dleon1919@yahoo.com). Please write "send me the UID links" or something similar on the subject line. I promise to respond to your e-mail with the links within a week. Also, feel free to write to me if you have any questions about this book, or just to let me know what you think of it. I love to hear from and communicate with my readers.

Acknowledgments

If I were to list all of the people that I feel contributed to my efforts to write this book, these acknowledgments could be as long as the book itself. So to keep this brief, I am only going to mention here those people I would not forgive myself for failing to thank. First, I would like to express my deepest gratitude to my parents, who, despite not always agreeing with me or understanding my point of view, always supported me in my efforts to pursue my goals and always created for their disabled son an environment where I could do just that. I would also like to express my thanks to my brother Cesar for helping me find a way to publish this book and share it with the world. Lastly and above all, I would like to thank the Force of Life that resides in me (and resides in all of us) for guiding me to this simple, reasonable, and satisfying understanding of how and why we exist.

Opening

When I was in college, I wrestled with wanting to commit suicide. The American dream – which I interpreted as the freedom and opportunity to achieve happiness through material prosperity and success – did not call to me, did not feel meaningful and worthwhile to me. And I felt very confused and troubled because, as the firstborn son of Cuban immigrants who came to the United States to escape communism, arriving with almost nothing and having to work very hard to become successful upper-middle-class American citizens, and who wanted their children to have similar ambition, I thought that there was something seriously wrong with me – particularly because I did not want what my parents had wanted when they were my age. It sounds silly to me now – silly that I would have considered committing suicide – but at that time I did not feel that I could be happy living the life that my parents wanted for me, or more specifically, be happy with what my parents wanted me to want. However, I knew that fundamentally my parents simply wanted me to be happy, so I held fast to the belief that as long as I was following my bliss, my parents would come to understand my choices. Thus without knowing exactly where following my bliss would take me, I chose to live in a way that I found fulfilling, allowing my curiosity and my bliss and my intuition to guide me. At the same time, I made it a strong priority to honor my parents by working very hard to follow my bliss without having to ask for financial help from them. Here is a poem I wrote many years later that expresses the struggle I went through at that time:

Taking to the High(er) Way

When I was young they used to say,
"Live your dreams. Don't let them stray."
Until they learned my dreams weren't theirs –
That I didn't care for cars or furs.

The comforts they would have me choose
Would forego truths I would not lose;
From common needs I sought release
To amplify my sense of peace.

"But then what will you do for money?
We just want what's best for you, honey."
But I hungered for things much more basic to live,
Things I soon learned all their caring couldn't give.

Money or not, we were all going to die.
What I needed most was a reason to try –
Something bigger than life to carry me on
And take me past death in an infinite dawn.

"I have to do this in my own unique way –
Whatever the pain, that's the price I'll pay –
And live my questions out to their end,
And hope that there they'll answers lend."

Some say I'm crazy, but I say it's them,
Who prize a doomed life like some precious gem.
It's true I don't know what I will meet,
But that beats living a dead-end street.

So living my questions out to their end moved me to study philosophy, anthropology, and linguistics, and, after college, moved

me to travel to Asia and Central America and Brazil to experience living in different cultures and learning foreign languages. I also read many books with a variety of ideas about life and existence and purpose, all the while continuing to allow my curiosity, my bliss, and my intuition to lead me and guide me. Then in my mid-thirties, during a time when I was starting a business combining tourism with English language instruction ("EST/English Study Tours" is what I called it), I had a disabling bicycle accident because I was one of those idiots who often rode their bicycle without wearing a helmet. After two brain operations and six weeks in a coma, I awoke to find that my life had been drastically changed. Little did I know that I had won the lottery.

Although my traumatic brain injury greatly affected my motor skills, my memory and reasoning ability were left completely intact. And although I spent a few weeks feeling depressed, after I changed my attitude and began to look for the bright side of the situation, things began to get better and better. That was over fifteen years ago, and the reason I say that I had won the lottery is because becoming disabled cured me of something that might be considered tragic and debilitating in its own way: busyness.

Of course, you might say, "What's wrong with always being busy?", and to this I would respond, "Well, inherently nothing. But depending on your situation, busyness could be a very damaging thing." For example, if being very busy distracts you from being a good spouse, it could easily lead to divorce. In my case, busyness was simply distracting me from discovering the true meaning and purpose of my life, and life in general. "So what?" you might say, "What's so important about discovering the true meaning and purpose of one's life?" Well, once again, inherently nothing... until you hit a wall. For example, if you suddenly get fired from a job that you have dedicated years and years of your life to or your spouse suddenly leaves you after many years of marriage, you might ask yourself "What have I been doing all these years?", and you might suddenly feel that your life has no meaning.

Before I became disabled I did not feel that my life had no meaning, because I had been living what I felt was a meaningful life since I graduated from high school and enjoyed the freedom to choose what I wanted to do with my life. But I still had questions. Becoming disabled freed me from the busyness of a typical life so that I had the time to organize my thoughts related to everything I had learned from my years of study and reading, and focus on forming sensible, reasonable answers to big questions that still haunted me, questions like "Who am I really?" and "Why do I exist?" and "What is my purpose?". And in my silent pondering, things began to become clear to me: reasons and explanations began to form in my mind, and I began to write them down. What started as a few pages of text to capture and organize the thoughts that were coming to me grew and grew and grew, and things began happening in my life that contributed to this text. I began to call my writings *Unity in Diversity: a new dawn* and described my text as a simple, reasonable and satisfying explanation of God and how and why we exist (it's all about love).

These ideas have allowed me to understand life and myself in a way that gives me great pleasure and joy. May they do the same for you.

The unexamined life is not worth living.
– Socrates

Unity in Diversity

a new dawn

The obvious is that which is never seen
until someone expresses it simply.
– Kahlil Gibran

If you can't explain it simply,
you don't understand it well enough.
– Albert Einstein

The thinking that we are
has brought us to where we have already been.
In order to go somewhere else,
we must think in a different way.
– Albert Einstein

We shall require a substantially new manner of thinking
if mankind is to survive.
– Albert Einstein

Introduction

By way of introduction, I simply want to say that the ideas I'm about to explore are nothing new. These ideas have been expressed in one form or another since biblical times (in other words, they appear in the Bible, although in a different manner) and even before that. And they are presently being discussed by many people other than myself, mostly by people connected to the New Age and spirituality movements.

I recommend that you at least read the first chapter (it should not take you more than around thirty minutes, as it is relatively short) before deciding that you are not interested in reading this. The worst that could happen is that you discover that these ideas make no sense to you, but if they do make sense to you, then you are in for a wonderful ride: an explanation of a beautiful way of viewing and understanding ourselves and the world. And I repeat: these ideas are nothing new. However, the way they are explained here is very new indeed.

1

Our Connection to God

Quantum physics, which studies the composition of atomic and subatomic particles, reveals that at an atomic and subatomic level everything interconnects, interrelates, and is interdependent. In 1993, Erwin Schrödinger, the Nobel Prize winner for physics, said, "Quantum physics thus reveals a basic oneness of the universe." This directly relates to how we are connected to God.

For this explanation to sound reasonable you need to believe that there is a force, energy, or power that, on the deepest, most basic level, is completely unified and whole and without divisions, which runs parallel to what quantum physics reveals. And that it unites and includes everything. I call this force/energy/power "God", and I assert that because at this most basic, all-inclusive God level there are no divisions or duality, there is no consciousness on that level of existence. Let me explain:

Consciousness (meaning "a cognitive state in which one is able to perceive and respond to stimulus") requires duality or contrast. For consciousness to be possible there needs to be a *see-er* (someone or something that sees) and a *seen* (someone or something that is seen): in other words, a duality/contrast. *Beingness*, on the other hand, requires no duality/contrast. Thus, there can be existence without consciousness.

Let me illustrate this difference between consciousness and being/beingness with a simple experiment that you can try for yourself. Put your hand in some still water (water that is not moving, like in a bucket or a sink or a bathtub), where the water is the same temperature as your body. Keep your hand motionless and do not touch any part of the container that is holding the water.

After a brief moment, you will sense that your hand has become one with the water and you will not be able to feel where your hand ends and the water begins. Specifically, you will sense that your hand still exists (that it is a part of your being), but you will no longer be conscious of it – it will feel like it has become one with the water because the contrast between your hand and the water will have dissolved. But once you move your hand (or simply clench your hand into a fist), you will begin to feel the friction of the water against your hand (or feel the friction of your fingers against your palm), and through this duality/contrast, you will become conscious of your hand once again.

This simple experiment illustrates very clearly how consciousness requires duality/contrast while beingness does not – beingness actually requires the absence of duality/contrast. I recommend that you perform this experiment to clarify this difference between consciousness and being if you do not clearly understand this difference already, because it is essential that you understand this difference to completely comprehend these ideas.

There are many instances in which we lose consciousness but do not cease to exist (do not stop being), such as while we are sleeping or under anesthesia in surgery. In these instances, consciousness is dissolved but of course we continue to exist (we continue to be).

On the all-inclusive God level there is no duality/contrast – only oneness or beingness. Thus, we can conclude that on that level God is not conscious. However, to say that God is not conscious is ridiculous because what we call "God" is supposedly omnipotent and capable of anything and everything (and please note that I am only saying that God is not conscious on that all-inclusive level; I am not saying that God is not conscious). So how does God experience consciousness?

Please pay close attention here because this is the crux of the concepts that I am trying to explain. In order to experience consciousness – specifically, to be able to experience consciousness of Himself/Herself – God divides Himself/Herself into pieces that appear to be separate from the whole in order to create contrast. This contrast allows for consciousness in the same way that, going back to the illustrative example of your hand in the water, moving or clenching your hand creates contrast and allows you to be conscious of your hand in the water. And we are those pieces, those conscious pieces. In other words, we are pieces of God that God has divided from Himself/Herself in order for God to experience consciousness, and God experiences consciousness through us. Yes, that's right: God experiences consciousness through us, or rather, *God is conscious through us.*

Hopefully, this explanation of how God experiences consciousness through pieces of Himself/Herself that have been divided from the whole, and the understanding that we are those pieces, can serve as a rational counterpoint for many New Age statements that are thrown around these days, such as "We are God/We are one with God/We are directly connected to God".

As I said in the introduction, these ideas appear in the Bible, although in a different manner. For example, Jesus called everybody his brothers and sisters, which implies that if Jesus is the son of God, then all of us are also the sons and daughters of God. So the belief that "We are directly connected to God" is not something that was first expressed through the New Age movement. Now let's explore this further:

So there is an all-inclusive but not conscious God level – an all-inclusive *being* level – that includes everything and is endless, eternal, and all powerful, that in order to consciously experience Itself, to "know" Itself, divides Itself into pieces and thus creates a reality, creates a realm, creates a level of existence where consciousness can exist: a reality defined by duality/contrast that we call "the world", that is in and of itself not endless and eternal but is the product of a power or force or energy and level of existence that is endless and eternal.

These two levels of existence – the all-inclusive being "God level" and the finite, duality-ridden "conscious level", where consciousness is possible – coexist interdependently in a sort of yin-yang relationship. Let me clarify what I mean by "yin-yang relationship" with the following explanation (and feel free to skip this short explanation if you are already familiar with this aspect of Chinese thought. I have bolded the relevant parts).

Yin and Yang, opposite and complementary forces in Chinese thought, from Chinese words meaning "shaded" and "sunny". Beginning in the early 4th century BC Chinese philosophers wrote about yin and yang in terms of the environment, especially the shaded and sunny sides of a hill. By the end of that century yin became associated with everything dark, moist, receptive, earthy, and female, whereas yang was bright, dry, active, heavenly, and male. Yin and yang were **believed to combine in various proportions to produce all the different objects in the universe.**

There is always an element of yang within yin and an element of yin within yang. Together they are symbolized by a circle divided into black and white sections, with a dot of white in the black portion and a dot of black in the white portion. This interaction indicates that **the characteristics of yin**

cannot exist without those of yang, nor the characteristics of yang without yin. Chinese philosophers stressed the importance of balance between the two to ensure social and political harmony. Rebellion, floods, and disease were said to be caused by an imbalance of yin and yang. Fortune-tellers and doctors in China and later in Japan advised governments and individuals on ways to restore harmony in relationship to yin and yang.

(Microsoft® Encarta® Encyclopedia 2003. © 1993-2002 Microsoft Corporation)

We exist as conscious beings because God creates us specifically to be able to experience Himself/Herself consciously. And our level of existence (the finite, duality-ridden, conscious level) is contrary to but dependent on the God level of existence (the all-inclusive being level) because without it, without God, it would not exist and thus we would not exist. And the God level of existence is also dependent on our level of existence in order to experience Itself consciously. In other words, without us God would not be conscious of Himself/Herself. This is why I say that these two levels coexist interdependently in a sort of yin-yang relationship.

As I said in the introduction, these ideas are presently being expressed by many people connected to the New Age and spirituality movements. For example, Neale Donald Walsh, the author of the popular *Conversations with God* books, says to God in a YouTube video titled "The Journey of Purpose" (go to the Internet address directly below to see this video for yourself, if you are curious), "What am I doing here?", and God answers (in response to this eternal question), "You exist in your present form that I might know Myself through you and through all of life." And that is exactly what I have just explained.

https://www.youtube.com/watch?v=QgRgZ7-1pZ0

Why is it that we get tired and need to sleep periodically in order to continue functioning normally? Could it be that maintaining the lie of individuality – which is a lie because we are actually parts of a unified whole that is God, although consciousness, which requires duality, would have us see ourselves as "individuals" separate from one another and separate from the world around us – is very draining and unfulfilling? Could this "lie" require that we submerse ourselves periodically back into all-inclusive being, which is our source, to recharge ourselves and gather the strength, satisfaction, and fulfillment needed to maintain this illusion of individuality? Here is a short poem that illustrates this:

Lullaby

Now I lay me down to sleep
To commune with what is deep.
Far beyond my thoughts I go
To a place I cannot know.
In sleep there is no consciousness,
Where thought divides and separates.
In sleep we drink of oneness,
And oneness is what satiates.

Or in the words of Deepak Chopra, "Sleep is very important because now we know that sleep is actually the way our soul refreshes our body." I heard him say this in a televised interview that he had with Oprah Winfrey: she was discussing the benefits of meditation with him when he said this about the importance of sleep in order to maintain physical well-being.

Our innate desire to evolve as human beings is due to the fact that the conscious level of existence does not satiate us and we hunger for the truths of the all-inclusive being (God) level of existence on which our conscious level of existence is based, truths that do satiate us. We feel naturally motivated to make our world, which exists on this conscious level, more like the all-inclusive being level/God level of existence. So we have been moved to eradicate slavery and racial inequality and promote gender equality, for example, because we feel naturally inclined to make our world more like the all-inclusive being level of existence. Specifically, we seek to make our world better reflect the qualities of the all-inclusive being level, where everything is unified and whole and where divisions and boundaries do not exist, and we continue to move in that direction.

It is interesting to note that many of the things that make us happy are related to overcoming differences or divisions. For example, making new friends and developing romantic relationships are both directly related to bringing together two things (people in this case) that were previously separate. Or so consciousness would have us believe. This type of happiness is directly tied to overcoming differences or divisions because deep down we yearn for union, we yearn to overcome divisions and yearn to feel beyond our conscious selves. Deep down we are aware that our conscious, duality-ridden "reality" is an illusion and that in the ultimate reality – the reality on which our "reality" is based and on which it is dependent for its existence and which is our true home – there are no divisions.

It is believed that "God is love" (at least that is what I was taught having been raised a Christian), but what exactly is "love"? Well, if God is love and God is a force/energy/power that is home to an all-inclusive level of existence, couldn't we say that love is the ability to see through duality and separation, and perceive the unity (the all-inclusiveness) that exists within diversity – within the duality and separation that seem so real in our world? In other words, isn't "to love" simply *the ability to see unity in diversity*? When we love, aren't we simply seeing through the illusory divisions and boundaries that come with conscious perception?

Or to put it in other terms, when we love aren't we simply perceiving with our hearts and souls instead of our eyes and minds?

Our own personal evolution, our own personal spiritual growth, is about learning to override or to see through the conscious illusions of divisions, boundaries, and separation that appear to be so real in our world in order to see the unity that underlies these illusions and to have the faith and courage to act from that. In this way, we are able to act from seeing unity in diversity, to act from love, in order to evolve beyond the lies and limits of our own egos. What follows is a poem about feeling the courage to do this, to act on believing in unity in diversity.

Of All That Hurts

Of all that hurts that I can find,
Nothing compares to this, simply:
To fit my soul within my mind
Is all that's really killing me.

To rip my feelings into words
And act from fear of losing love,
To live among untrusting herds
Ignoring callings from above,
Is more than my soft heart can bear –
Is worse than any other pain –
And leaves me much too numb to care.
Such normalcy cannot be sane.

But what else is this world about?
What else can a person do?
These sorts of things my mind cries out –
These sorts of things and others too.

I understand one thing for sure:
To live the life my mind conceives
Is not so grand nor sweet nor pure –
Cannot compare in any way
To all these depths my soul believes.
And damn to hell what thoughts may say.

2

Human Diversity

It may seem strange that human beings can appear to be so differ-ent when we are all fundamentally the same – or just all different pieces of the same all-inclusive, unified being. However, accord-ing to a wonderful book about the variety of human personali-ties (*Please Understand Me II* by David Keirsey), the varieties of human personalities that exist are due to how we prioritize the following different aspects of consciousness (of our conscious selves):

- We are either more *introverted* or more *extroverted*.
- We are either more *sensing* or more *intuitive and introspective*.
- We either focus more on our *thoughts* or more on our *feelings*.
- We either prefer to *perceive* the world around us or to *judge* the world around us.

(Please be aware that *we all* have *all of these traits*, but that it is in how we prioritize these traits that creates our unique personalities.)

According to this wonderful book, which uses a seventy-one-question questionnaire to determine a person's specific personal-ity type, one's personality type depends on how one prioritizes these areas of one's consciousness. For example, I am more of an extroverted, intuitive and introspective, feeling, perceiving type of person, which, according to this book, means that I have an idealistic, communicative, cooperative, altruistic, and mystical personality. You can complete this questionnaire for yourself online to see which general personality type you fall under, and you can also read a description of your general personality type there (just go to the Internet address directly below), but if you want to read a description of your specific personality type, they will charge you for that, so I recommend that you find a copy of this book at your local library so that you can complete the questionnaire and read a description of your specific personality type at no cost to you.

http://keirsey.com/sorter/instruments2.aspx

Keirsey's book describes sixteen specific personality types in all. These different personality types exist because of the different ways we prioritize different aspects of consciousness, and combined with the variety of physical variables, psychological variables, cultural variables, ethnic variables, and personal experience variables that exist in our world, they are the reason why we all appear so different from one another although we are all fundamentally the same (since we are all pieces of the same all-inclusive, unified being). You could say that the source of our existence is like a beam of light that shoots through a prism – in our case, that shoots through a prism of physical/biological matter – to create a rainbow spectrum of colors or a wide variety of conscious beings. In other words, humanity represents a rainbow of conscious beings who all share the same source. How cool and beautiful is that?

3

Meditation

In the deepest spiritual sense of the word, meditation is an effort to turn off one's internal dialogue (the constant dialogue one maintains with oneself) in order to allow the deeper, unified being reality that lies within each of us to come to the surface. Through meditation, we learn to experience that we are one with the world: we learn to more directly experience that our conscious existence occurs within a greater unified existence that is beyond consciousness, the same way that we feel that (going back to the hand in the water illustration of experiencing the difference between being and consciousness) our hand is one with the water when the variables that allow us to see contrast are shut down. More specifically, when we turn off our internal dialogue and simply wallow in being, we become more clearly aware of a silent, peaceful realm that surrounds and engulfs our conscious existence, from which inspiration and intuition and divine guidance spring. Reaching "enlightenment" through meditation is, to put it simply, a matter of learning to see through the lie of conscious, duality-ridden experience and existence in order to strongly connect with, reside in, and operate from the all-inclusive God level of existence (the silent, peaceful realm that surrounds and engulfs our conscious existence). This enables us to become one with God in the same way that the hand becomes one with the water in my aforementioned illustration.

For those of you who have never experienced turning off your internal dialogue while awake, I strongly recommend that you learn how to meditate in order to experience the peace that comes from the silence of not having to put up with incessant mind chatter. As you learn to meditate more deeply, you will also experience the field of unified being that lies just beyond/beneath/past conscious existence in a more direct manner than simply through sleep.

There are many ways to learn how to meditate, so please continue searching until you find the meditation technique that works for you; do not feel that there is only one way to learn how to meditate and that if you cannot learn how to meditate using one technique, you will never learn. Just keep searching until you find the meditation technique that works for you. After you have learned how to meditate well, you should be able to turn off your internal dialogue at will whenever you wish, similar to being able to turn off a light switch. And it is very refreshing to be able to do that.

4

Evil

What we call "evil" is nothing more than an obsession with one's ego/individuality and acting out of a desire to promote or build on that obsession. That is to say, obsession with our own ego sense of individuality – specifically, feeling separate from others and acting in ways that prioritize and glorify this "individuality" – is the only real evil that exists. And the only real "devils" that exist may well be individuals who have an exaggerated self-importance, who truly see themselves as separate from others and act on behalf of this exaggerated but illusory belief in being separate.

Our own perception of ourselves as individuals separate from others is at the root of the evil that maintains the lie of duality and separation, which in turn makes our world "a living hell". And a world in which people believe that they are separate from others may well be the only hell that actually exists. Of course, there are scales and varieties of evil, but at the root of all types of evil is the belief and conviction that one is separate from others.

5

Death

Human beings appear to represent the pinnacle on the scale of consciousness through organic existence and we have a very refined sense of consciousness – a much more developed sense of consciousness than other organic beings. We also have a very strong tendency to falsely believe that we are independent beings separate from one another. That is the negative side of consciousness. Although there are advantages to consciousness, including knowledge and all that knowledge entails, the negative side is that because consciousness is something that requires a dual medium, as conscious beings we are inclined to believe that we are separate from others, from the world around us, and from the realm of unified being that is our source, our home, and ultimately, our final destination, otherwise known as "death".

Death is simply the end of an illusion. You see, we come into existence as pieces of God that have seemingly been separated from the whole of God (the unified field of all-inclusive being) in order for God to experience consciousness. But our duality-ridden conscious existence is an illusion because fundamentally we are not individuals separate from one another and separate from God: it is our consciousness that creates the illusion of being separate, of being individuals. At death, our physical organisms are no longer able to maintain our conscious beings, and the lie of our individuality dissolves along with consciousness. Then we revert back to that field of unified being – call it Heaven if you wish – that is at the root of our conscious existence.

Fundamentally, death represents the end of the illusion of our individual conscious existence and a return to God, to the field of all-inclusive, unified being, also known as "love", or in religious terms, "Heaven", which we had never really left to begin with – although consciousness made it appear that way, leading us to believe that we were independent beings separate from our source. This reminds me of this spiritual quote: "We are souls having a physical experience." In other words, we are not ultimately physical entities that have souls, but rather we are ultimately spiritual entities (souls) that have physical bodies.

This view of death may not sit well with people who prize their individuality and believe that their individuality will carry on beyond this life. To those people I would simply like to say that the part of you that is beyond your individuality will carry on and continue to exist as it has always existed. However, the playground that is conscious existence will only carry on through others: through other pieces of God that have been separated from the whole in order for God to experience Himself/Herself through conscious existence. It is important to understand that these "other pieces" that will carry on experiencing conscious existence are also you at the deepest level of your being, because everything is one on that level of existence. So actually, you – but not "you" the conscious individual, the ego – will continue to experience conscious existence.

Another way to view death is simply to see death as the cure to the disease called life. To appreciate this point of view, you need to imagine that you are viewing life from the perspective of the soul: you need to imagine that you are viewing conscious existence from the perspective of all-inclusive, unified being, which is our home. So in all-inclusive, unified being we find ourselves at peace, at ease, but when we incarnate as conscious beings, we experience the illusion of duality and separation and we feel diseased, which means that we experience the opposite of ease, we experience a lack of ease – we experience dis-ease. So at death, we return to the realm of all-inclusive, unified being and our dis-ease is cured. Shouldn't that be something to look forward to?

However, just because death is the end of an illusion or the cure to the disease called life does not mean that life is an illusion that we should disregard. While we are in this "illusion", it is very real, and we should treat it with the regard that it deserves. You might say that what we call "life" is "God's playground": it is the illusory medium in which God experiences Himself/Herself consciously (*playfully* experiences, you might say) in order to more fully experience Himself/Herself. And although it is an illusion in that the dualities it portrays are not valid in the true reality that is at the root of it, it is nonetheless real within its boundaries.

We vicariously experience joy and disappointment through victories and losses in athletic game competitions, but we know that these "victories and losses" are an illusion – they are simply a product of the game. Nonetheless, we play the game seriously and follow its rules. In a similar way, life is also a game (and consequently, an illusion. Or as the popular nursery rhyme goes: "Row, row, row your boat, gently down the stream. Merrily, merrily, merrily, merrily, life is but a dream."), but its rules need to be followed within the limits of the game while we are alive as conscious beings. Also, we need to respect God's playground and not run it into the ground. We need to take care of our bodies and our planet out of respect for God so that God can continue to consciously experience this wonderful world He/ She has created.

Here are two poems that clarify death:

Walking on the Beach, Like Waves

Walking on the beach while young,
My skin made brown from so much sun,
I kicked the waves and walked the sands,
The warmth of summer in my hands.

But now I walk the beach anew –
My steps are slow, my thoughts are too –
And smile for that child I once was,
Removed by time (as time so does)
And wonder at this motion, still,
Of waves and sand and life's lone will.

How could I have outrun the tides –
Exceed my source with all my strides?
But they have not forgotten me:
I'll too, like waves, return to sea.

And Soul Remains

Like some great ocean that I swim,
There is a power that I reap:
Something eternal deep within
That I partake of when I sleep.

Nearer than my beating heart,
Closer than my silent pleas,
Lies in me this unseen part,
Because it is the thing that sees.

This ancient home beyond my mind,
Wherefrom all my callings drift –
Nor harsh nor sweet nor cruel nor kind –
Awaits the lie called me to lift.

> Still and silent, patiently,
> Watching all the things I do,
> It swallows all that I call me,
> And sole remains when me is through.

I would like to share something interesting that a college roommate told me about that relates to why we may suffer at death. He was telling me about a book he read in which raccoons were trapped and caught through the use of shiny objects placed in holes in logs. More specifically, a shiny object (like a crumpled piece of aluminum foil) would be placed in a hole that had been drilled into a log, and then a few nails would be hammered around the hole in such a way that the tips of the nails would be protruding through the walls of the hole and pointing toward the shiny object in the hole. Attracted by the shiny object and led by a desire to take the shiny object from the hole, a raccoon would stick its hand into the hole and then, by grasping the shiny object, would make a fist, which got its hand stuck behind the nails. Of course, the raccoon could simply release the shiny object and unmake its fist to maneuver its hand past the nails and from the hole, but its desire to possess the shiny object would keep it trapped.

I found this interesting because it serves as a good analogy for how our desire to maintain our individuality (like the raccoon's desire to possess the shiny object) keeps us trapped in this lie of existing as individuals separate from one another and from God. And just as the raccoon suffers upon the arrival of the trapper because its desire to possess the shiny object keeps it from escape, many of us suffer upon the arrival of death because our desire to maintain the lie of individuality keeps us from abandoning our thoughts of being separate from everything in order to freely, of our own volition, return to God: to the unified field of existence, to the unified field of all-inclusive being, where individuality and duality do not exist.

We need to get over ourselves, we need to stop being so consumed with our egos, to truly feel connected to God – to all-inclusive, unified being – which is our source and our destination. In this way, we will not experience loneliness nor fear of death.

The popular saying that goes, "the bigger they are, the harder they fall", in relation to these ideas could go, "the more you cling to ego, the greater your eventual suffering". This is because the ego is an illusory, transient phenomenon that we relinquish at death, whether we want to or not.

But why should it be that we have to wait until death in order to return to God? Why should we have to wait until we are dead to rest in peace – or rather, to be at peace with our own existence? If we learn to abandon our thoughts of being separate from everything, we can feel united with God, feel as if we have returned to God, feel completely immersed in love, and be at peace long before our deaths. Here is a poem that expresses how I have come to find peace in my own life:

Stand

I tried to walk my parents' road,
Thinking they'd know what's best for me,
But could not justify the load
Nor do things I did not believe.

I walked my generation's road,
Thinking it'd be what's best for me,
Until discovering that their load
Was but a masked conformity.

I took an independent road,
Thinking I'd sense what's best for me,
And followed intuition's load
Beyond accepted sanity.

I found myself upon a road,
A quiet road that carried me,

Unburdened me of all my load
And all my thoughts of what should be.

I realize now my life's a road,
A road upon an inner land,
That cannot predefine its load,
And where it goes is where I stand.

I have been told by a friend who is a nurse and has often been in the presence of dying people that most people do not appear to suffer upon the arrival of death. The ones who truly suffer are the loved ones of the deceased. But why do they suffer? It is primarily because they are focused on the ego bonds that they have with the deceased instead of focusing on the deeper bonds beyond their egos that unite them, not only with their deceased loved one, but with everyone. Here is a poem about that connection we have with others that defies death:

To Reach a Friend

If I built a bridge to you,
Would you build a bridge to me?
Past time and space – just for two –
A bridge across eternity:
Across the lives that we have led;
Across the tears that we have shed;
Across the things we'll never tell;
Across whatever private hell;
Across the trials that fate may send;
Across, with hope, to reach a friend.

But bridges burn and bridges rot.
Bridges across eternity can not
Unite whatever love we share
For too long or with much care.
For just as life gives time to play,
Life, in time, takes all away,

But that ocean and that ground
Where our souls embrace unbound.

So let our bridges burn and fall:
Try to save them not at all.
Let life take them all away –
Dreams to dust is what we pay –
Leaving what is deep to bear
All the love that we would share.
And when our hearts rest in that place,
In that vast eternal space,
No need to bind, no need to pair,
Dust sprung from love that's everywhere.

Remember that obsession with our egos – with our "individuality", or rather, our "I-dividuality", and the belief that we are separate from others – is the only true "evil" that exists. This evil is what we must fundamentally overcome in order to live peacefully with one another as a human race and is also what each of us needs to overcome to see the unity in the diversity of our world, in order to see love and to love more fully, and to be truly happy and at peace. Here is a poem that reflects this theme:

Destiny

Trees rise high up from the grass;
Birds fly whistling as they pass;
And little critters in the ground
And skies and lakes and all around...

Even clouds know where to go,
And shifting winds from whence they blow,
And planets floating far away
Spin on in their own magic way.

All these things all have their place
And dance with their own private grace,

Without question, doubt, or fear
As to how or why they're here.

And so too our human race
Must flow within designs of grace
And live out its humanity:
That each of us traverse our "me".

6

Animals and Consciousness

Regarding whether animals experience consciousness or not, they do experience consciousness, though much more subtly, in a much less refined way, than human beings do. Once again, I define consciousness as simply the ability to perceive and respond to stimulus, and given this definition, even plants experience a degree of consciousness because they can at least respond to the direction from which they are exposed to light. Given their high degree of experiencing consciousness, it can be said that animals also represent "pieces of God" that have been separated from the whole of all-inclusive, unified being, and probably experience a closer connection to God (to all-inclusive, unified being) as a result of a less heightened conscious individuality.

In other words, because animals are less grounded in consciousness, they are much more intimately connected to the state of being that exists beyond consciousness. This is why some animals often appear to be more loving than many human beings. Animals also suffer less at the loss of life. Since they experience a lower degree of consciousness and consequently have a less refined sense of individuality, they don't feel as strong a sense of loss upon losing their lives and whatever sense of conscious individuality that may have come with it.

7

Our Purpose

I have already discussed why we are here ("We exist as conscious beings because God creates us in order to experience Himself/ Herself consciously..."), and now I would like to discuss a related topic: the purpose of our lives.

The purpose of our lives is to glorify God, but not in the religious sense. We glorify God (all-inclusive, unified being. Not the old bearded man in the sky, which is a religious image of God) by bringing to the conscious level the truths of the all-inclusive, unified being level that is at the base of the conscious level of existence. We best glorify God by dedicating ourselves to making our world a better reflection of the truths of the all-inclusive, unified being level of existence on which it is based. I discussed this a little when I wrote, "Our innate desire to evolve as human beings is due to the fact that the conscious level of existence does not satisfy us and we hunger for the truths of the all-inclusive being (God) level of existence on which our conscious level of existence is based...". Simply put, our purpose is to glorify God by creating a heaven on Earth, a place where love rules absolutely.

God is moving us to transform this conscious world into a heaven: to transform our division-riddled world into a place that directly reflects the truths of the all-inclusive, unified realm of existence that is at its base. To a large degree, we have been doing this for thousands of years – since we came into existence as conscious beings. We best do God's bidding by tuning in to the part of ourselves beyond our consciousness and beyond our individual needs and desires, to act from a source of motivation that serves us all – as opposed to simply serving our individual needs and desires.

Of course, nobody can tell you what God wants you to do but you yourself; only you know what your intuition (which is your instinctive knowing without the use of rational processes) is telling you to do. In biblical terms, it's like we each have Satan whispering in one ear that we should do what makes us happy in the form of pursuing personal gains that would give us advantages over others (that's the conscious, division-oriented part of ourselves speaking: our ego), and we also have an Angel whispering in our other ear that we should do what makes us happy in the form of pursuing goals that make us feel more united with others (that's the deeper being, union-oriented part of ourselves speaking: our heart and soul). And we are each caught in the middle trying to do what "makes us happy", but may not be completely clear about what that is.

Hopefully, these ideas will help you understand that struggle and see how important it is for you to glorify God by choosing appropriately to pursue goals that better reflect the ultimate, unified reality that is at the base of our existence: by choosing love. Choosing appropriately is the only way we will truly find peace. Here is a poem to inspire you to choose appropriately:

What's Coming

Life will squash you like a little bug
Or crush your fears upon the ground of love,
Will beat you slowly far into despair
Or gently spread your heart out everywhere,

Will blind you with bright light till your eyes sting
Or help you see yourself in everything.
The difference between bliss and agony
In all the things you hear and feel and see
Is to know the tune that life is humming
And accept with grace in you God's coming.

It is important to adhere to the rules and heed the requirements of this conscious existence we call life. I want to make it very clear that I am not suggesting that we should stop pursuing personal gains that are social requirements in order to live a happy life, fulfilling our needs for food and shelter and so on. However, we have to realize that if having some things makes us happy, having more and more of those things *does not* necessarily make us more and more happy. Greed only serves to achieve a reasonable level of material happiness, but excessive greed does not necessarily lead to more happiness.

We need to judge for ourselves when our desire for more is serving our needs to maintain our physical existence in order to serve God, to glorify God, or whether our desire for more is simply serving our devilish belief that more is better – that if some can make us happy, then much, much more will make us much, much happier. That is not at all true. If it were true, then rich people would notoriously be the happiest people on Earth. And that is not the case, given the fact that some of them actually commit suicide because they are so unhappy.

While writing this, I came across a program on PBS by bestselling author and teacher Dr. Wayne Dyer titled "Five Wishes Fulfilled Foundations". In this program he expresses ideas that run parallel to ideas that I express here, as well as this sharp summation:

"You can either be a host to God
or a hostage to your ego."

We can either live from the sense of all-inclusive, unified being and listen to the Angel that is telling us that we should pursue goals that make us feel more united with others, or we can believe in the lie of duality and separation and be a hostage to our ego's desires to pursue personal gains that would give us advantages over others (often at the expense of others). This urge to shift priorities is being felt by more and more people these days. Here is a poem that expresses this phenomenon, that a revolution is taking place, a revolution that with this poem I call "A New Dawn":

A New Dawn

Silent rain on silent seeds
Is waking up once silent needs:
In each of us, deep in our hearts,
Is where the silent growing starts.

When we have had enough of things,
A deeper yearning in us stings,
And as our pain moves tears to flow,
This very rain makes new things grow.

Out of the ground where we'd felt lost,
Among the hopes that we had tossed,
Where old roots wind a worn-out course,
New growths reach out from some new source.

Then slowly we begin to feel,
As leaves turned toward the sky implore,
A sun is shining now for real
That we had only dreamt before.

Our conscious selves would like us to believe that we are in control of our lives, but beyond our thoughts, we know better. We feel it when we are suddenly attracted to someone or something (a place, an idea, a plan) in a way that may be beyond reason, and for an instant, we feel like puppets on strings. It is in those moments that God acts through us to shape our lives and our world – which are actually His/Her lives and world – to better reflect Him/Her/Love.

I have felt this way in writing this book: that this book is God's doing. God is moving us all toward another great transformation of our world, and it's time for all of us to wake up and listen to God, to have faith and be brave and trust that God knows what God is doing when we feel moved to do something seemingly ridiculous or crazy, such as to write a call for transformation with the intention of redefining ourselves, our existence, and our world. I will end this chapter with another poem that I wrote (that God moved me to write), which expresses this theme.

Twenty-First Century Mantra

A million years we walked afraid
To touch with hands that love has made:
Love's heart put deep inside our soul,
As if within an endless hole.

Afraid to bridge eternity,
We moved along ever slowly,
With hope our only guiding light
To spur us on our inner flight.

Faith in the rain, faith in the sun,
Faith in the plants and beasts we'd won,
Searching for what to call our own...
But each step left us more alone.

We've worshiped kings, God's sons on Earth;
We've worshiped things imbued with worth.
We've fought for bragging rights to God,
Then rights to Earth once that felt odd.

Through all the years our sense has grown
That nothing we can call our own,
But open hearts and granted trust
Can build a heaven out of dust.

Now is the time: we hear love calling
What is ours in each of us.
The time has come: this is the dawning
Of the Age of Aquarius.

For those of you who are unfamiliar, I want to explain that the last two lines of this poem are in reference to the message in a popular song from the 1960s (and considered by many to be the quintessential song of the 1960s American New Age movement) called "The Age of Aquarius". Go to the Internet address directly below to watch and listen to a video of this song, if you are curious.

https://www.youtube.com/watch?v=kjxSCAalsBE

Directly below are the lyrics of this song so that you can read its message to see how it relates to the poem above, if you are curious about this.

When the moon is in the seventh house
And Jupiter aligns with Mars
Then peace will guide the planets
And love will steer the stars

This is the dawning of the age of Aquarius
Age of Aquarius
Aquarius
Aquarius

Harmony and understanding
Sympathy and trust abounding
No more falsehoods or derisions
Golden living dreams of visions

Mystic crystal revelation
And the mind's true liberation
Aquarius
Aquarius

When the moon is in the seventh house
And Jupiter aligns with Mars
Then peace will guide the planets
And love will steer the stars

This is the dawning of the age of Aquarius
Age of Aquarius
Aquarius
Aquarius
Aquarius
Aquarius

Let the sun shine
Let the sunshine in
The sunshine in

Let the sun shine
Let the sunshine in
The sunshine in

Let the sun shine
Let the sunshine in
The sunshine in...

8

Our Greater Purpose

I received an e-mail from a personal growth organization called the Silva Life System™, which regularly sends me information about their products, and this message from them stands out in particular as it contains information that directly relates to our "greater purpose" and how that greater purpose guides us in our lives. Here is what it says:

You've heard people tell you...
"You can achieve anything, and be anything you want to be."

But if that were true, why aren't you, at this very moment, enjoying the success, wealth, health, happiness and enlightenment you've desired all your life?

Could it be that you're not motivated enough? Are you unprepared?

Do you lack the proper guidance?

Perhaps.

But there's an even bigger culprit that most people don't know about...

Many self-improvement systems and organizations will claim that as long as you can imagine it, you can have it.

This is correct to an extent – but it's not entirely accurate.

Because the truth is, you can only experience true success when your actions are in line with your greater purpose.

You see everyone is put on this planet for a reason – whether to help others, inspire others, or simply to spread joy.

And when you discover what YOUR reason is, doorways will open for you.

Obstacles will melt as if by magic. Positive coincidences will occur.

Inspiration, motivation and positivity will flow from your very being...

And before you know it, you'll be living a life of unbreakable purpose, deep satisfaction and profound happiness.

Finding your greater purpose is easy when you learn to listen to your intuition.

It teaches you how to train your mind to unleash the intuitive abilities within. It will automatically program you not only to find and identify your life purpose, but also to attain it.

As Jose Silva once said, "The reason we are given psychic (intuitive) ability is so we can use it to get information from higher intelligence to find out what we are supposed to do, and how to do it."

This e-mail from Silva also contained a link to a webpage with a video that reflects the message above and also explains what Silva recommends to help you find and pursue your greater purpose, but apparently this video has since been removed from the webpage. Nonetheless, a brief message on the webpage also relates to the subject of our "greater purpose", so I would like to share it with you. Here it is:

The Surprising Reason Dreams Sometimes Don't Come True

We want to be clear about something. You are absolutely entitled to have every success, happiness and fulfillment you can dream of. This is a common truth for everyone – including you. But here is the one problem that many people find themselves in. According to Jose Silva, they try to achieve what they think they should do, instead of what they were sent here to do.

All of us are destined for a greater purpose, a purpose that serves our whole, that serves to help make our conscious, division-ridden reality a better reflection of the all-inclusive, unified being reality, as opposed to serving our ego-driven greed and the lie of a division-based reality. We can access this greater purpose by learning to listen to our intuition. In the words of Osho:

"Each person comes into this world with a specific destiny – he or she has something to fulfill, some message that has to be delivered, some work that has to be completed. You are not here accidentally – you are here meaningfully. There is a purpose behind you. The whole intends to do something through you."

We are like trees, each destined to produce a particular, unique fruit or seed to contribute to the world. And like plants we all need to face toward the sun, which in our case means intuitively connecting with our source – with the all-inclusive, unified being reality... with God – in order to grow our fruit, in order to live in line with our greater purpose and magically fulfill the purpose that we came into conscious existence to fulfill. Here is a poem with a message that is directly related to this theme:

Dear Sun

You're so pretty in the sky –
No brighter, richer love I've found.
And I have looked – you know I've tried:
I've searched far and high this ground.

And I am not the only one
Who turns to you harmoniously:
So many creatures worship sun
To bathe in warmth more nakedly.

Dear Sun, I've got a problem here.
You see these paths that man has made?
I've tried them all – plain, without fear –
Searching in them for what I've craved.

But none fulfills me, none sustains,
Nor motivates me to renew
This urge to share deep in my veins
That you, above all else, imbue.

The only one that calls is you –
Your light, your heat, your openness –
But my life is yet far from through,
And I'm not moved to make it less.

I've just one question, if you please.
Let's say I set my sights past man:
Let's say I start to live like trees,
Reaching toward you all that I can.

Would you tell me what to do
With all these years that aren't yet through –
Make sure they're lived pure and true –
If I surrender them to you?

Not to sound like a broken record, but all of our fruit (all of the purposes that we came into conscious existence to fulfill) are related in some way to serving to make our conscious, division-ridden reality a better reflection of the all-inclusive, unified being reality, to creating a heaven on Earth, in whatever way possible – even maybe in a seemingly inconsequential way. If you feel drawn to anything written here, that might just be a sign that your deeper self is trying to find understanding – it might just be God's spark in you trying to guide you to a greater understanding of yourself so that you may go on to fulfill your greater purpose with more clarity and faith.

It is time for more and more of us to wake up and listen to what God put us here to do; it is time to turn on the lights and turn up the love. Following is a poem to inspire you to do just that.

Just This

We're not from another star
But we have come from very far
To trace an image in this place,
With sweat and blood and tears, God's grace.
The power that has made us so
Beyond our needs drives us to grow
And teaches what we must unchoose
To strip away what we must lose
To realize where we are from
And then undo what we have done
To cloud the waters of this place
That have obscured from us God's face.

9

Social Change

I feel that God guides my life, and more accurately according to these ideas, that God lives through me in order to experience, affect, and transform this world so that it better reflects Himself/Herself/Love. I know that you might think that I sound like a lunatic, but more and more people are doing things to bring these sorts of ideas to the surface.

For example, Tom Shadyac, the director of successful Hollywood blockbusters such as *Ace Ventura: Pet Detective* and *Bruce Almighty*, in 2010 made a very interesting documentary film called *I Am*. The film opens with this wonderful quote by Ralph Waldo Emerson:

> The world is his,
> who can see through its pretension...
> See it to be a lie,
> and you have already dealt it its mortal blow.

Tom Shadyac is a successful Hollywood movie director and *I Am* is his story: a story he says is about mental illness, but it is only about mental illness in a very broad sense (you will see what I mean if you watch this film). Something happened that forced Shadyac to rethink his priorities and moved him to make this documentary film, instead of his usual comedy films. As a result of a bicycle accident in which he broke his hand, he suffered a nasty concussion that turned critical when he developed a condition called post-concussion syndrome (more commonly known as shell shock), which is a mild form of traumatic brain injury in which the symptoms sometimes do not go away for months and even years, if ever. Feeling that he was facing his own death brought an instant sense of clarity and purpose. Shadyac asked himself that if he was indeed going to die, what did he want to say before he went? It became very simple and very clear: he wanted to tell people what he had come to know. And what he had come to know was that the world he was living in was a lie.

After months of isolation with no contact with the outside world, suddenly and unexpectedly Shadyac's post-concussion syndrome symptoms began to recede, which was very odd and somewhat magical because all of the conventional medicine and alternative treatments he had tried had all proved unsuccessful with regard to treating his symptoms.

When he had improved enough that he could tolerate travel, Shadyac grabbed a camera, put together a film crew of four, and began to spark a conversation around these two challenging and rarely asked questions:

What's wrong with our world?
What can we do about it?

This is a very interesting film that runs parallel to the ideas that I am writing about here, and I highly recommend it to those of you who are interested in reasonable, intelligent answers to those questions I cited above. However, for the purposes of this chapter, I only want to mention some things that are said in parts of this film.

Approximately thirty-three minutes into the film, the topic of how animal groups come to decisions is explored. For example, how does a group of deer in a pasture decide on which watering hole to go to and when to go to it? It had long been believed that the alpha male of the group would be the one to make such decisions, but it was surprisingly discovered that these animals came to decisions in this way: once 51 percent of the group decided on a common, definite course of action, the entire group would instantly adopt that course of action. In the case of the example of the group of deer, once 51 percent of the group began facing and motioning toward a specific direction, toward a specific watering hole, the entire group would suddenly and unanimously adopt that course of action and the entire group would head toward that watering hole. And in many cases, the alpha male would be left standing behind wondering what had happened and where everybody had gone.

The film then goes on to conclude that cooperation and democracy are programmed into animal DNA (and thus into our DNA). Later in the film, it's also pointed out that human beings over time became the dominant species, not because we are stronger or faster or bigger, but simply because we are the species that has best learned to cooperate with one another and take care of one another. According to Darwin, sympathy is the strongest instinct in human nature, which means that sharing the feelings of others – feeling connected to others or feeling one with others or feeling that there are no divisions between you and others or being able to love – is the strongest instinct in human beings.

Another interesting thing that is said thirty-seven minutes into this film refers to when Darwin wrote about human evolution and sexual selection in *The Descent of Man* in 1871, which is not the work that initially made him popular – that was *On the Origin of Species,* which is about his theory of evolution, and was published in 1859. In this book (*The Descent of Man*), Darwin mentions "survival of the fittest" twice and he mentions the word "love" ninety-five times (granted, he probably felt that he had mentioned survival of the fittest enough when he wrote *On the Origin of Species*). In *The Descent of Man* Darwin talked a lot about behaviors like conciliation and cooperation. However, Darwin was interpreted and popularized by Thomas Henry Huxley (an English biologist), who had a much gloomier view of human nature and really stressed the idea that the natural world was an anarchy of the strong treading the weak. And that is how the idea of survival of the fittest and the belief that selfishness and aggressiveness dominate in the animal kingdom became popularized – which popularized the erroneous extension of these thoughts by using them to justify that this is why selfishness and aggressiveness are natural to humanity, are simply "human nature".

So Darwin was historically interpreted by people who ignored the aspects of love, conciliation, and cooperation that were intrinsic to Darwin's ideas, and that is why these days Darwin is more closely associated with the idea of survival of the fittest. But you can see that survival of the fittest was not Darwin's most central idea concerning animal or human social development.

I am bringing up the film *I Am* and this 51 percent decision-making principle primarily because it reminds me of something I had learned about in college when I was studying philosophy, anthropology, and linguistics. In one of my anthropology classes, I learned about something called "the hundredth monkey theory" that states the following (I have bolded the important parts, but you will need to read the entirety to completely understand it):

The Hundredth Monkey
A story about social change.
By Ken Keyes, Jr.

The Japanese monkey, Macaca Fuscata, had been observed in the wild for a period of over 30 years.
In 1952, on the island of Koshima, scientists were providing monkeys with sweet potatoes dropped in the sand. The monkeys liked the taste of the raw sweet potatoes, but they found the dirt unpleasant.

An 18-month-old female named Imo found she could solve the problem by washing the potatoes in a nearby stream. She taught this trick to her mother. Her playmates also learned this new way and they taught their mothers too.

This cultural innovation was gradually picked up by various monkeys before the eyes of the scientists. Between 1952 and 1958 all the young monkeys learned to wash the sandy sweet potatoes to make them more palatable. Only the adults who imitated their children learned this social improvement. Other adults kept eating the dirty sweet potatoes.

Then something startling took place. In the autumn of 1958, a certain number of Koshima monkeys were washing sweet potatoes – the exact number is not known. Let us suppose that when the sun rose one morning there were 99 monkeys on Koshima Island who had learned to wash their sweet potatoes. Let's further suppose that later that morning, the hundredth monkey learned to wash potatoes.

THEN IT HAPPENED!

By that evening almost everyone in the tribe was washing sweet potatoes before eating them. The added energy of this hundredth monkey somehow created an ideological breakthrough!

But notice: A most surprising thing observed by these scientists was that the habit of washing sweet potatoes then jumped over the sea... Colonies of monkeys on other islands and the mainland troop of monkeys at Takasakiyama began washing their sweet potatoes.

Thus, when a certain critical number achieves an awareness, this new awareness may be communicated from mind to mind.

Although the exact number may vary, this Hundredth Monkey Phenomenon means that when only a limited number of people know of a new way, it may remain the conscious property of these people.

But there is a point at which if only one more person tunes in to a new awareness, a field is strengthened so that this awareness is picked up by almost everyone!

(From the book "The Hundredth Monkey" by Ken Keyes, Jr.)

It is fascinating that the 51 percent decision-making principle is so similar to this hundredth monkey theory (because they link group decision making and social change to a kind of democratic telepathy). I wanted to mention them because maybe you believe that the ideas expressed here are worthless, but first of all, more and more people are beginning to spread ideas similar to the ones expressed here, and secondly, if democratic telepathy is valid then these ideas will soon become common knowledge when enough of us (51 percent of us) begin to believe in and act on these ideas. So don't give up on these ideas or on living through unity in diversity just because you feel that one person cannot make a difference, because one day enough "one persons" will make all the difference, and everything will click and we will all be in tune with and living out these ideas. Yes, one day! And speaking of one day...

10

"One Day" and Serendipitous Coincidences

It's magical how much serendipity and coincidence have played a part in writing down and developing these ideas. It's like that message from the Silva Life System says: "You see everyone is put on this planet for a reason – whether to help others, inspire others, or simply to spread joy. And when you discover what YOUR reason is, doorways will open for you. Obstacles will melt as if by magic. Positive coincidences will occur. Inspiration, motivation and positivity will flow from your very being..."

Writing this has been for me a magical journey full of serendipitous coincidences. For example, recently I received an e-mail from an e-pal in Brazil with a link to a very inspiring music video titled "Kindness Boomerang" that starts with this message: "life vest inside: because kindness keeps the world afloat". This video is accompanied by a very hopeful song called "One Day" and the lyrics are perfect to share with you here because they beautifully complement what I am writing and specifically this hundredth monkey theory, as if to say "One day when enough of us believe... then all of us will believe...". Directly below is the Internet address to this video followed by the lyrics of this song.

http://www.youtube.com/watch_popup?v=nwAYpLVyeFU& vq=medium#t=77

Sometimes I lay
Under the moon
And thank God I'm breathing
Then I pray
Don't take me soon
Cause I am here for a reason
Sometimes in my tears I drown
But I never let it get me down
So when negativity surrounds
I know some day it'll all turn around
Because
All my life I've been waiting for
I've been praying for
For the people to say
That we don't wanna fight no more
There'll be no more wars
And our children will play
One day [x6]
It's not about
Win or lose
Because we all lose
When they feed on the souls of the innocent
Blood drenched pavement
Keep on moving though the waters stay raging
In this maze you can lose your way
It might drive you crazy but don't let it faze you no
way
Sometimes in my tears I drown
But I never let it get me down
So when negativity surrounds
I know some day it'll all turn around
Because
All my life I've been waiting for
I've been praying for
For the people to say

That we don't wanna fight no more
There'll be no more wars
And our children will play
One day [x6]
One day this all will change
Treat people the same
Stop with the violence
Down with the hate
One day we'll all be free
And proud to be
Under the same sun
Singing songs of freedom like
One day [x2]
All my life I've been waiting for
I've been praying for
For the people to say
That we don't wanna fight no more
There'll be no more wars
And our children will play
One day [x6]
Ooooooooooooooooooooohhhhhhhhhhhhhhhhhhhhh

11

Avatar and What Is Happening on Earth

Even the movie *Avatar*, which was extremely popular, is about a conflict that directly relates to ideas expressed here. This movie is about a conflict between an aggressive people who want to manipulate a group of indigenous people on their foreign planet in order to gain access to their land. More specifically, they want to relocate this group of indigenous people so that they can have better access to a very expensive mineral that exists in high concentrations on the indigenous people's planet.

But this movie could also be interpreted as being about a group of ego-oriented people who believe that they are separate from the world around them – specifically, that they are separate from their environment, which is why their home planet has decayed considerably, although the movie does not explore or explain that much but only alludes to it because that is not the primary focus of the film – and who believe that they need to manipulate and control the world around them through aggression and technology, that are in direct conflict with a group of people who feel that they are one with the world around them and that everything is connected to everything else, and is connected to a great, beautiful and all-loving source.

So what happens? Well, to put it simply – and there is much more to the story than this – although the aggressive people's technology is very powerful, the indigenous people of the planet come together cooperatively with one another and with the animals of the planet to defeat their greedy and aggressive foe. At the height of the conflict, their divine source awakens many seemingly unconnected conscious beings of the planet (people and animals alike) to come together and achieve victory. In the last scene of the movie, the main character, who was a member of the aggressive people's society but infiltrated and became a part of the indigenous people's society through the use of an avatar body (you really need to see the movie to understand what I mean by "avatar body"), is completely reborn in his avatar body and leaves his other body for good. More specifically, he leaves his ego-oriented self and fully commits to a self that feels one with the world and connected to everything else, including a great, beautiful, and all-loving source.

Consider that the *Avatar* story runs parallel to what is currently happening on Earth. Our ego-centered greed preys upon our environment, and by acting on this greed, we appear to be slowly destroying our environment, our planet and, ultimately, ourselves. So will our divine source awaken us in time to defeat our own ego-centered greed before we destroy our planet and ourselves?

More and more of us appear to be waking up to the fact that we need to make some drastic changes if humanity and our planet are to survive, and this urge to wake up is coming from our divine source, from the spark of unified being deep within each of us.

12

A Clean Conscience and Making a Difference

A clean conscience is essential to be at peace with oneself. To be able to love, admire, and respect oneself it is essential to believe that you are living in a way that conforms to your own sense of what is right – that you are living with a clean conscience. After all, the person you spend the most time with is yourself, so it is very important to be able to love, admire, and respect yourself in order to feel at peace.

Your sense of what is right might be greatly influenced by your society, your family, your religion and your spiritual beliefs, and your knowledge of the world around you, but it is crucial that you make the final decisions regarding what is right because, in the end, you are the only one who truly and unavoidably has to live with yourself.

And it is important to keep a clean conscience on all levels of your being: your physical being, your psychological being, and your spiritual being. For example, if you are gaining weight and you are unhappy with that, and your conscience is telling you to learn about what you need to avoid eating in order to avoid becoming overweight, then you need to make an effort to learn about that in order to maintain a clean conscience (in order to be at peace with yourself) because, otherwise, you will only have yourself to blame for your physical unhappiness as a result of becoming overweight. And the same goes with your thoughts and emotions and your spirit: you need to keep a clean conscience in those areas, otherwise, you may experience unhappiness in those areas also.

When it comes to a clean conscience, ignorance is bliss. For example, if you consider yourself an animal lover and you abhor the terrible things people do to animals but you are a meat eater and know nothing about terrible things done to animals to produce the meat you eat, then not knowing about those things keeps you in bliss. However, the moment you learn about terrible things that are done to animals to produce the meat you eat, you are no longer ignorant and your conscience may demand that you change your eating habits in order to keep itself clean, in order to allow you to live at peace with yourself.

Of course, hypocrisy is rampant and many people choose to ignore their conscience or to manipulate their conscience and modify their own sense of what is right. But it takes effort to ignore or manipulate one's conscience, and that kind of effort often does not allow one to feel good about oneself. Peace with oneself has to be earned: it is earned by keeping a clean conscience.

Staying ignorant makes it easier to keep a clean conscience and to be at peace with yourself, but what's the fun of having a sports car if you can't drive it fast? Specifically, what's the fun of having an evolved brain if you can't use it to learn and become more educated about yourself and the world around you? And do you think your conscience would allow you to keep your brain in first gear? Yes, having a clean conscience is hard work, but isn't being at peace with oneself worth it? Or would you rather be dependent on things that allow you to escape yourself and ignore your conscience? That's hard work too.

Do you ever wonder why people make an effort to improve the world or help others? Well, every person has their own reasons, but essentially it comes down to keeping a clean conscience:

they do what they feel motivated to do, what they feel enthusiastic about, because they feel that they need to live in a way that conforms to their sense of what is right in order to be at peace with themselves. So why bother making an effort to improve the world or help others? The answer is simple: to keep a clean conscience; to live and sleep well without having to depend on medication or other things to help you sleep or allow you to live peacefully with yourself.

Are you doing everything you can to keep your conscience clean in order to be at peace with yourself? Are you comfortable with the direction the world is taking? Is your conscience begging you to do something about it?

You are not powerless to influence the world around you. Like that "Kindness Boomerang" video illustrates, every little act of kindness affects our world positively, sometimes creating a chain reaction that sparks a wave of kindness. And please be aware that with every dollar you spend, you are voting. For example, you are either voting for processed foods or for whole, natural, possibly organic foods. You are either voting for fossil fuel consumption or for the use of alternative transportation energy sources. You are either voting for more aggressive, violent films, or you are voting for whatever kinds of films you choose to enjoy. And on and on. So act and choose wisely.

In the words of Jane Goodall:

You cannot get through a single day
without having an impact on the world around you.
What you do makes a difference,
and you have to decide
what kind of difference
you want to make.

13

Heaven and Hell

I remember reading something interesting many years ago illustrating the difference between Heaven and Hell. It went something like this:

Imagine that after you die you are reborn in the afterlife but without elbows. In Hell everybody is miserable and starving because they sit at a table with food but cannot bend their arms to put the food into their mouths. In Heaven everybody is happy and satisfied because they sit at a similar table with the same food as in Hell but are all feeding one another.

Maybe the difference between a heaven and a hell is the simple difference between disregard for others due to obsessed ego-oriented self-concern, and living cooperatively. Let's learn to "feed one another" with each act and each choice that we make in order to transform our world into a heaven.

14

Connecting with Our True Selves

On May 20, 2012, OWN (the Oprah Winfrey Network) broadcast a show called "Finding Your Authentic Power with Gary Zukav" in which Oprah interviewed Zukav regarding a topic which fits perfectly with what is written here. I first became familiar with Gary Zukav when I read his book *The Dancing Wu Li Masters* while in college, and I loved it because it made quantum physics sound like mysticism, and I always considered myself a bit of a mystic (someone who believes in the existence of realities beyond human comprehension).

Approximately five minutes into the show, Oprah asks Zukav to explain the soul, and what follows is his response. (This is not a complete verbatim transcription of this part of that interview, but only includes what is relevant to the subject of connecting with our true selves.)

"The soul is not a mythical entity", Gary says. "The soul is a powerful, purposeful essence. The soul is that part of us that existed before we were born and will continue to exist after we die. It's that part of us that is immortal. And it's that part of us that has the intentions of harmony and cooperation and sharing and reverence for life. The soul is your mother ship, so when you're sailing in the same direction that it wants to go, your life fills with meaning and purpose, and when you sail in another direction, it empties of meaning and purpose. You can look at it this way: You are a personality. That means you were born on a certain day and you'll die on a certain day: ashes to ashes; dust to dust. But your soul won't die. Your soul is you also. We're on a journey to the soul – you could put it that way – while we're here in this span between birth and death. And while we have this precious opportunity to walk on the Earth, the question becomes: What will we do with this personality? What will you do with you? Now here we can define 'you' in a couple of ways. One is you with a little 'y' – the personality that was born and then will die. The other you is the You with a big 'Y' – that's your soul. And if you use your time while you're on the Earth to align the little you with the big You, your life begins to fill with meaning, fill with purpose, fill with joy. And you know why you're alive: to follow what you know your soul wants you to do."

And Oprah says, "Oh, when my personality comes to fully align with the energy of my soul and I allow my soul to be the guide, then that is when I am the most powerful. That is when I am in what I call now 'my sweet spot'!"

And Gary says, "You were born to live in the sweet spot. That is the creation of authentic power. And that's how we're all evolving now."

"That everybody was born to live in the sweet spot." Oprah says.

"Yes, yes." Gary says. "There's been a huge change in human consciousness that has occurred, and its ramifications are going to be felt and the experience of it is going to be felt by everyone."

"You think so?" Oprah asks.

"Yes, I do." Gary says. "What I'm talking about is this: I'm talking about an expansion of your perception beyond the five senses, beyond what you can see and taste and touch and hear and smell. As people become multi-sensory they begin to become aware, to sense in some way that there is a big 'Y'."

"A big 'Y'." Oprah says.

"A big 'Y'." Gary says. "A mother ship. Something that is meaningful. And millions of us are acquiring that sense – that sense that life has a meaning. That I have a purpose. That I am more than this mind and body: I am more than molecules and dendrites and neurons and enzymes. I have a part of me that is immortal. Now the question becomes: What now?"

"What now?" Oprah says. "All right, Gary, now that we know that, what now?"

"That is for each of us to decide." Gary says. "Multi-sensory perception does not make us more kind or patient or caring or less angry. It makes us more aware. And when you get that sense, the spiritual work begins, because how do you do that? Well, the answer (to the question 'What now?') is elegantly simple. You find the parts of your personality that don't want those things (that don't want to fully align with the energy of the soul and allow the soul to be the guide), you become very familiar with them so that you can recognize them when they come up in you, and you don't act on them. And you find the parts of your personality that do want those things (that do want to fully align with the energy of the soul and allow the soul to be the guide), and you recognize them and you become very familiar with them, and when they come up in you, you act on them. And that's how you create authentic power.

Creating authentic power is developing the ability to distinguish between love and fear within yourself and then choosing love, no matter what is happening inside of you or what is happening outside of you."

I primarily wanted to share that with you here because I feel that Gary gives a very clear explanation regarding connecting with our true selves: aligning our personality with the energy of the soul and allowing the soul to be our guide. Our personality lies in the realm of consciousness, the realm of thoughts – in the mind. But our soul lies in the realm of all-inclusive, unified being, the realm of inspiration and intuition – in the Divine. The mind and the soul must work together in order to experience true bliss (in order for your life to fill with joy and meaning and purpose). The mind is a magnificent tool, but it has a limited perspective (because consciousness requires duality/contrast, which makes us inclined to see things as separate), and the soul has a much wider perspective but you cannot negotiate physical life and conscious existence from only that perspective. We must learn to balance the mind – reasoning and rationality – and the soul – inspiration and intuition – to experience true bliss.

In the words of Albert Einstein:

**The intuitive mind is a sacred gift
and the rational mind is a faithful servant.
We have created a society that honors the servant
and has forgotten the gift.**

(If you enjoyed reading my transcription of part of that interview and you would like to read more of Gary's thoughts, I strongly recommend that you pick up Gary's book, *The Seat of the Soul*.)

15

Change and Social Revolutions

I have had doubts about whether what I am being moved to write will have any effect on making the world a better place, on changing the world by sparking a social revolution. I have suspected that these ideas will only sound meaningful and significant to people who, like me, have intuitive and introspective, feeling, perceiving types of personalities. Specifically, I have had my doubts about whether these ideas will have any effect on people like my parents, who are not particularly interested in a new, reasonable way of understanding ourselves and our world.

But I am okay with that because, first of all, it takes all types of personalities to make a world; I am not inclined to question my faith in the belief that every person, that every uniquely distinct personality, is here for a reason. And secondly, it only takes enough of us...

As illustrated in that 51-percent decision-making principle and the hundredth monkey theory, it only takes enough of us to get these ideas before everybody (or most everybody) starts to feel that they get them. However, it takes time for people to come around. For example, during the time when most people believed the world was flat, it was not the case that somebody (one person) finally came up with a reasonable explanation for the world being round and not flat, and then suddenly everybody started to believe and act like the world was not flat: started to sail ships beyond the horizon without fear that they would fall off of the Earth. It takes time for thinking to change. And here is a more modern example:

In North America well before the United States had been formed (in 1619, to be more exact), European settlers believed that it was acceptable and a necessity to have people from Africa as slaves. But finally enough people decided that this would no longer be tolerated and in 1860 (more than two hundred years later) Abraham Lincoln, an anti-slavery president, was elected, which prompted eleven southern states where slavery was practiced to move to secede from the Union. However, the federal government would not accept this (would not accept the secession of these states from the Union), thus sparking four years of warfare that Americans call the Civil War.

But liberating African Americans from slavery did not mean that they were suddenly treated with equality. The Civil War ended in 1865, but it was not until the 1960s (one hundred years later) and the height of the civil rights movement that blacks began to be recognized as equal citizens by the federal government. And still there were (and still are) stubborn personality types who regarded (and still regard) African Americans as less than equal to white Americans.

Furthermore, for those of you who are too young to know (I am also too young to know this, but I learned about this from my favorite linguistics professor, a feminist from Utah who had been raised by Mormons), women were not allowed to vote in the United States until 1920.

It takes time for society and people to change, and we should not lose hope because we have come a long, long way already. Some people may never come around, but I am okay with that. It just takes enough of us to come around in order to change the status quo so that what was once strange or inconceivable becomes completely normal, acceptable, perfectly believable, and obvious.

Social revolutions are like trees:
fragile and vulnerable at birth,
but almost invincible once they have matured.

16

A New Dawn

A new dawn is upon us: the pain we feel from witnessing, and often experiencing, the horrors and tragedies stemming from how we mistreat and disregard our world and one another drives us to wake up and change our course. This new dawn is moving us to more fully shift from an "I" based consciousness, which views the self as separate and distinct from the whole, to a "We" based consciousness, which views the self as including everybody, and our environment, and moves us to act from a source of motivation that serves us all. To expedite this shift and more smoothly experience this new dawn, we must, as a global community, learn to communicate more effectively with one another and learn to feel more united.

Money is the blood that flows through the circulatory system of commerce that feeds the muscles (individuals that act and produce) that keep our world in motion (growing and improving). To effectively bring about this new dawn, we need to create financially viable structures to strengthen communication and community on a global scale. To serve this need, I propose three practical projects we can develop to turbocharge our evolution, together. The following three chapters describe these projects.

17

My English Childhood

To facilitate communication and understanding on a global scale, it would be extremely conducive to share a common language. However, some of the bloodiest wars have been between opposing sides that spoke the same language (I am specifically referring to civil wars), so having a global common language will not guarantee world peace. Nevertheless, making it easy for people to learn a global common language will allow individuals – individuals who want to be part of a global community interested in communicating with one another to promote understanding in order to prevent and disrupt global conflicts and build world peace – to more easily join the global community. In case you were not aware, English has become the international language; people are not only interested in learning to use English in order to communicate with people from English-speaking countries – they are interested in learning to use English in order to be able to communicate with people from all over the world. Imagine if almost everyone in the world could speak a common language. How much more quickly could we learn from one another and how much better could we learn to understand our differences and how much more effectively could we work on solving our problems? Just imagine.

There is a great need for a central website to help the world learn English. We need to make it easier for people around the world who have a desire to learn English (especially people who cannot afford to pay for English classes or do not have the time or ability to go to English classes) to effectively learn English using a computer and an Internet connection. Above all, we need to make it easier for people around the world to learn the language that has become the world's common language if we want to more effectively learn to understand one another and peacefully coexist. Such a website could help people learn English in order to communicate with a person from another country, to more easily understand books, articles, videos, and films designed to share information on a global scale, or to get a job in which the ability to communicate with people in English is a requirement. Given that there is such an obvious great need for such a website, you might think that such a website already exists. Actually, there are already many websites that help English language students learn English or improve their English, but none that can teach a student who is completely unfamiliar with English to become completely fluent in English. In other words, there is not an English-learning website out there that is complete.

I propose that we create a website similar to YouTube, with a huge library of videos to which people could also contribute their own videos, to teach the world English. The essential requirement would be that all videos be in English with perfect closed captions (with text in English so that people could see the written form of what is being said on the videos in order to be able to teach themselves to read English while they are learning to understand spoken English). Each video could be labeled with a short text in English explaining what it contains or what it aims to teach. And the videos could all be categorized into levels of English, possibly fifteen levels: five basic levels, five intermediate levels, and five advanced levels. This way, people using this website to learn English or to improve their English could easily find videos that correspond to their level of English proficiency.

The videos should be relatively entertaining to make learning English fun.

A series of level 1 videos could be created titled "My Infancy" with the "My Infancy: crying" videos showing a baby crying and the parents saying things like "Why are you crying? Are you hungry? Do you need your diaper changed? Mommy is coming. It's your turn to feed the baby now." And the "My Infancy: first words" videos could show a very young child saying their first words and first statements in different situations, like asking for food or a toy or for their mother to pick them up. Another series of level 1 videos could be created titled "My Youth" with videos labeled "My Youth: kindergarten" and "My Youth: first grade", et cetera, showing a child using English in different situations throughout their youth.

And another series of level 1 videos titled "English Classroom" could be about a classroom of a few English language students from around the world with a teacher who is a native speaker of English. This classroom could be in New York or Miami or Los Angeles or Seattle or London or Sydney, or any other international city where English is spoken. The "English Classroom in New York: self introductions" video could show the teacher introducing herself by saying "My name is Susan. I am from New York. I am an English teacher." and then asking each student to stand up and introduce themselves in the same way. And an "English Classroom in New York: asking others basic questions" video could show the teacher teaching the students to ask and answer the questions "What is your name? Where are you from? What do you do?" and request that all the students stand up. Then she could ask one of the students the three questions and after the student answers the three questions correctly, with her help, she could sit down and tell the student to ask another student the three questions, and then sit down. Then that student who answered the three questions would ask another student the three questions, and then sit down. All of the students would have an opportunity to answer and ask these three questions, and then sit down. This way the students watching the video could learn these basic questions and learn about the characters (the teacher and the students) in the "English Classroom in New York" series of videos. The English Classroom videos could teach basic English in a classroom setting and in settings outside of the classroom showing the teacher taking the students to visit a park or a supermarket or a department store or the teacher's home or well-known places in the city where the class would take place. And storylines incorporating the background of the students could be created to make the videos more entertaining and teach different aspects of English in context. A series of English Classroom videos could be created for children, for teenagers, and for adults to cater to the interests of these three distinct age groups. And these English Classroom series of videos could evolve into intermediate and advanced level videos.

Specific videos could also be created to help teach specific vocabulary, like body parts, and types of food, and days of the week and names of the months, and specific grammar, like irregular verbs and how to use different verb tenses to talk about the past, present, and future, and comparative and superlative adjectives, and other aspects of English, like phrasal verbs and prepositions, et cetera. And these videos could be categorized into the level that corresponds with the English Classroom videos that begin to incorporate the vocabulary and grammar taught in those videos.

And a series of videos titled "My Life" could be created in which people talk about different subjects, such as, for example, "My Life: what I do every day" and "My Life: what I did yesterday" and "My Life: how I met my husband" and "My Life: my job as a policeman" and "My Life: my next vacation", et cetera, to show people talking about different aspects of their lives in the present, past, and future. And people around the world could submit their own "My Life" videos to show what their lives are like in different parts of the world. All of the videos that are submitted would be reviewed by the My English Childhood submissions department to check for English accuracy and closed captions accuracy and to determine the level of English they correspond to before being approved and added to the My English Childhood library of videos. As you can see, this library of videos with the goal of teaching the world English would contain videos from people all over the world not only for the purpose of teaching English to the world, but also to teach people around the world about people and places around the world.

A special series of level 1 videos could be created for children using cartoons and characters that regularly appear in the cartoon videos. Imagine if the Walt Disney Company produced a series of videos to teach English to children using Disney characters and locations in the Disney parks around the world to post on this website. Children around the world could enjoyably learn English on a computer and visit Disney parks through videos while learning what to say in English in Disney parks around the world. If we made English fun to learn on a computer for children, imagine how many children around the world could at least learn to understand basic English before they turn 10. Imagine what a sense of belonging to a global community who speaks the same language this would inspire in these children.

And the great thing about teaching and learning English (or any language) is that you don't just need to talk about English when you are teaching and learning English – you can talk about anything. So "My Life" intermediate level videos could be created to teach children how children live in different parts of the world. For example, a video could be about a girl who lives in Shanghai talking about herself and her home and her family and her city, and videos could be created about children living in different parts of the world to teach children how children in the rest of the world live. It would be a very enjoyable way for children to learn about other parts of the world while learning English. And children from different parts of the world could contribute videos to this website to share information about where and how they live with other children learning English in other parts of the world. Imagine the possibilities.

Videos from other English language websites could be submitted to this central English language website by the people who run those websites similar to the way that many videos that exist on independent websites are uploaded onto YouTube. These videos from other websites would be rated and given a label before being added to this huge library of English language study videos.

And this website could be called "My English Childhood", because what essentially distinguishes native English speakers from non-native English speakers is that native English speakers have had a childhood in which learning to communicate in English was essential to be able to interact with the people around them, so native English speakers have a memory bank of English interactions and conversations to draw on when speaking English. This website could offer a memory bank of English interactions and conversations that non-native English speakers could study to create in their minds their own English childhood.

For students wanting to bridge the gap between an advanced level of English proficiency and becoming comfortably fluent in English, a series of level 15 videos could be created labeled "NSLCP/Native Speaker Listening Comprehension Practice" consisting of videos of movie excerpts and videos of TV shows, and even videos of entire movies. For example, an "NSLCP: movie excerpt from *Casablanca*" video would show an excerpt or a scene from the movie *Casablanca* with perfect closed captions to help the student understand everything being said on the video, and an "NSLCP: episode of *Friends*" video would show an episode of the popular American sitcom *Friends* with perfect closed captions to help the student understand everything being said on the video. And for students interested in being able to understand entire movies in English, perfect movie scripts (movie scripts that perfectly represent what is being said in the movie) could be offered to the students (for free or at a reasonable price) so that students could download the movie script of a movie they want to be able to understand perfectly and completely to study this movie script in order to understand it completely before watching the movie again and again to perfect their English listening comprehension skills. This way, English language students could learn to understand the spoken English used in specific situations (as shown in movies and TV shows) to create a great memory bank of English interactions and conversations to draw on when speaking English in order to become fluent in English.

Imagine a website with entertaining videos (even cartoons) that children could watch to learn English through watching fun videos from a very young age. We could teach most of the world to understand English in one generation.

Or imagine that you are an adult who decides that you need to learn English in order to get a better job or simply to be more qualified to do the job that you already have, but you are very busy and do not have the time nor the means to study English at a language school in your city. So you search the Internet looking for websites that could help you learn English. You discover the My English Childhood website and the first thing you see is a webpage that says "Click here for an explanation of how to use this website to learn English or improve your English." in your native language, and many other languages. So you click on the link, and this opens a webpage with an explanation in your own language of how to use the My English Childhood website to learn English or improve your English. And on this webpage there are advertisements and announcements about bilingual dictionaries (in English and your native language) that you can use online or download from the Internet or purchase in your country to help you with your English studies, and there is also an area of announcements by English teachers who speak your native language offering their services to help you improve your English via e-mail or Skype.

These dictionary advertisements (and other advertisements appearing on the website) and other announcements would not be free and would generate funds to make the My English Childhood website profitable in order to pay the salaries of the people who make the My English Childhood website possible. And the My English Childhood website could also have a staff of qualified English as a second language teachers that students could communicate with via e-mail to practice and improve their written English skills or via Skype to practice and improve their oral English skills at reasonable prices.

Remember that the goal of this website would be to effectively teach the world a common language. And although English language schools around the world might think that it will put them out of business, English language schools could actually use the My English Childhood videos as part of their curriculum. They could create a room with computers that have access to the Internet where students could spend time watching and studying My English Childhood videos that their teacher assigns them to watch and study, and then the students could practice what they learn from these videos in the classroom with their teacher and the other students in their class.

Think about it: with such a website anybody in the world (at least anybody with a computer and an Internet connection, and the desire and motivation to learn to communicate in English) could learn English. What would the world be like if everybody in the world could speak a common language? Just imagine.

18

The Internet Payment Network

Imagine that you are a teenager in Brazil (or in any country where there are young people who are eager to learn English) and you have been teaching yourself English using books and videos but now you would like to interact with a native English speaker in order to practice and improve your pronunciation and conversation skills. However, the English language schools where you live are expensive, and you are just a teenager who does not have a job (you just do whatever you can to earn some spending money, like yard work and washing cars and babysitting, et cetera). So what can you do?

You can search through the classified ads section of the My English Childhood website to look for an announcement by a native English speaker willing to give English language instruction either for free or at a reasonable price. You can then contact this possible English tutor via e-mail to discuss the details. Let's say that you first want to practice your spoken English in order to improve your English pronunciation. So you communicate this desire to the English language instructor to see if this person would be willing to help you with this. Now let's say that this English language instructor wants to charge $10 per hour for this language instruction via Skype (which is less than a native English language instructor in your city in Brazil would charge). How are you going to pay this person who lives in another country?

You could pay them using the Internet Payment Network (the IPN). Of course, the IPN does not yet exist, but this is how it could work when it does exist:

First, you would need to open an account at the IPN branch in your country. You could do this in person (if there is an IPN branch in your city) or you could do it online (by registering on your country's IPN website). You would need to deposit funds into your IPN account before being able to send payments from your IPN account to another person with an IPN account. You could also do this in person, or you could mail a check to the central IPN branch in your country. Although you do not have a checking account, you could give your parents (or any person you trust who has a checking account) $40 of your personal savings (of the money you have earned doing whatever) and ask them to write you a check for $40 made out to the Internet Payment Network so that you could deposit the funds into your IPN account and send a payment to your online English language instructor (this person would also need to have an IPN account in order to receive your payment). However, you could not send your online English language instructor more than $40 because that is all that you have in your IPN account. In order to be able to send more than $40, you would need to deposit more money into your IPN account.

Such a network would make it possible for people who do not have a credit card or a bank account (specifically, young people) to pay for goods or services around the world. The initial goal of the IPN is to create a network which would allow people who want to give or receive online instruction to be able to pay or receive payment for this online instruction in a way that does not require a credit card or a bank account (which is what PayPal requires). However, this payment network could be used by individuals to pay for or receive payment for all kinds of services they give and receive from other individuals around the world via e-mail or Skype. For example, a young person who is confused about their sexuality because they find themselves sexually attracted to people of the same sex but does not want to speak with their parents about their confusion could search online for a psychologist familiar with this kind of trauma and would be able to pay this person for online counseling using the IPN. And the IPN could also be used to pay for goods sold by companies that have an IPN account.

The IPN would be unique in these ways:

- No credit card or bank account would be required to be able to open an IPN account. You would simply need to have a mailing address at which you could receive withdrawal checks from your IPN branch when you choose to make a withdrawal (unless you are able to make withdrawals in person, in which case there would be no need to mail you a check).

- You could only send payments using the IPN in amounts that would be covered by the balance in your IPN account. You could not send money that you do not already have in your IPN account.

- Although a criminal could use a person's IPN account number and personal identification number to make illegal and unauthorized purchases, this criminal would not be able to spend more money than the person whose IPN account this criminal is using has in his or her IPN account.

To keep things simple, the currency of the IPN would be the US dollar (unless the people who work together to make the

IPN a reality decide that another currency would be more suitable). So when opening an IPN account in a country that is not the United States, the funds to be deposited into the account would be converted to US dollars at the then-current exchange rate (and withdrawals would also be converted from US dollars to the currency of the country of the person who is making the withdrawal). This also means that all individuals and companies seeking payments through the IPN would have to set their prices in US dollars.

This Internet Payment Network would make it possible for people to make payments, receive payments, and transfer money in a variety of situations. Following are some examples.

A young English language student in Saudi Arabia (or any country where there are young people eager to learn English) could purchase a bilingual dictionary from a publisher that advertises its bilingual dictionary on the My English Childhood website with funds from their IPN account.

A Russian English language teacher in Moscow who has just had a baby and cannot continue working in a classroom because she needs to stay home to take care of her child and decides to teach English from home on her computer could advertise her services on the My English Childhood website and receive payments from the students she teaches online at her IPN account.

A college student in China who is getting a degree in English in order to become an English language teacher and who has studied English since they were a child and speaks advanced level English could earn money by posting an announcement on the My English Childhood webpage that explains how to use the My English Childhood website in Chinese, and invite Chinese English language students who would like help with their English from an

English language teacher who speaks Chinese fluently to contact the Chinese English teacher for help, and this Chinese English teacher could receive payments from the students via the IPN.

A young Indonesian woman who meets a young Australian man traveling in Indonesia and accepts his invitation to live in Australia with him in order to continue their romantic relationship there could go to Australia and send money she earns from working in Australia back to her parents in Indonesia using the IPN.

A young entrepreneur who is starting their own business and needs help from a graphic designer to design a logo for their business could search for a graphic designer online and then pay this graphic designer, who could be anywhere in the world, using the IPN.

These are just some examples of situations in which people could use the IPN, and there are many more situations in which people could use the IPN to pay for goods or services provided by individuals and businesses around the world, as well as transfer money.

The Internet Payment Network would need to be profitable in order to compensate the people who would make the IPN possible – to be able to pay them salaries – and thus it would need to charge for some of its services. So to open an IPN account, you would need to pay a $5 fee and there would be a $2 annual fee to maintain your IPN account (these are just possible prices). There would be a $1 charge in order to send a payment from your IPN account, but there would be no charge for receiving a payment. There would be a $2 charge for withdrawals from your IPN account requiring a check to be sent to your mailing address in the amount of your withdrawal, but there would be no charge for withdrawals made in person.

There would also be a limit on the amount of funds that one can have in their IPN account because, after all, the IPN is not a bank. And other rules would need to be created, such as a rule that states that if the annual fee is not paid then the $2 annual fee would automatically be deducted from one's account, and that if the account does not contain the $2 necessary to pay the annual fee then the account would be closed.

As you can see, this Internet Payment Network would make it possible for individuals (especially young people) around the world to pay for services that merit compensation offered by other individuals around the world and also to receive payment for services that merit compensation offered to other individuals around the world. And this ability to be able to compensate others for their help and to be able to receive compensation for helping others could motivate individuals to help others in innumerable ways. In this way, we could "feed one another" in order to move towards transforming our world into a heaven.

19

The World Without Walls

Every generation stands on the shoulders of the previous generation allowing it to see ills that the previous generation was blind to or simply saw as "the way things are", and innovations contribute to every new generation's efforts to heal the ills that the previous generation condoned. The development of spoken language, written language, the printing press, the telegraph, the telephone, the cell phone, the personal computer, and the Internet have in turn contributed to the growth of relationships, communities, cooperation, understanding, and knowledge to overcome the ills that have in turn plagued humanity since human beings evolved from animals by developing heightened consciousness. And heightened consciousness has been a blessing and a curse. It has been a blessing because heightened consciousness allows for the creation of thoughts, ideas, and knowledge, but it has been a curse because heightened consciousness requires duality/contrast, which makes us inclined to see ourselves as separate from one another and from the world around us, and most grievously, as separate from God – from all-inclusive, unified being – which is our source, our home, and our final destination. This illusory belief in being separate, from one another, from our environment, and from God, is what we must ultimately overcome to transform our world into a heaven, and we can use the innovations of the personal computer and the Internet to create a "world without walls" to move toward transforming our world into a heaven, into a world of beings with heightened consciousness that reflects the truths of all-inclusive, unified being, which is at the base of our conscious existence.

The World Without Walls (the WWW) would be an online international community created to help bring people together as a global family for the purpose of promoting world peace, happiness and belonging (specifically, promoting happiness from a feeling of belonging to a peace-loving global family). It could be considered the first online country so that people who are members of this community could state "I am a citizen of the World Without Walls" or, more simply, "I am a citizen of the World".

To become a citizen of the World you would need to go through an application process: you would need to apply for citizenship. This application process would consist of filling out an online questionnaire for you to show that you can effectively communicate in English, a request for you to explain why you are interested in joining the WWW, and a pledge for you to read and accept that states that you are dedicated to promoting world peace through the creation of a united, global family, and that you are aware that you could lose your citizenship for doing anything to another person that constitutes a violation of human rights.

Upon the approval of your application for citizenship, you would need to create a citizenship ID (for example, your citizenship ID might be "American man in NYC, 1999") and a password that you would use to access your citizen page, and you would need to submit information about yourself and an optional photo that would be posted on your citizen page. Your citizen page would show your photo (or photos, or simply an icon showing that you are male or female) and basic information about yourself that you would like other citizens to be able to see, and also your tags, that you could change at any time.

From your citizen page you would be able to search for other citizens and send them messages, and you would also be able to receive messages from other citizens in the inbox on your citizen page. For example, you could search for citizens that live in a place that you plan to visit, such as Paris, because you want to learn from someone who lives in Paris about the best farmers markets in Paris, so you search for "citizens in Paris who know about farmers markets" and a list of links to the pages of the citizens who have any of these words as tags would appear, and then you could look through the citizen pages of these citizens to determine if any of them would be able to inform you about the best farmers markets in Paris. And after finding a citizen in Paris that you think might be able to help you, you could send them a message from your citizen page using their citizenship ID and they would receive your message in their inbox on their WWW citizen page.

From your citizen page, you could also search for citizens who might be willing to help you in a variety of ways, from informing you about themselves and where they live to helping you learn about a specific subject that they consider themselves knowledgeable about that is included as one of their tags. For example, if someone considers themselves very knowledgeable about the history of their country they could have a tag that says "French history/Chinese history/Colombian history/et cetera" so that other citizens interested in communicating with a person who knows a lot about the history of their country would be able to contact them to request to communicate with them about what they know.

This is what you would see on the World Without Walls homepage:

ONE WORLD – ONE FAMILY!

Welcome to the World Without Walls! The World Without Walls (the WWW) is an international, English-speaking online community created to help bring people around the world together. Members of the WWW – called citizens of the World – can communicate and build friend-ships with people around the world using the WWW to learn from one another and learn about one another and interact with one another in order to raise the awareness that we are all part of the same global family, and to move towards solving problems caused by lack of under-standing so that we can experience more happiness as a united global family.

Click here to apply for citizenship.
Log in here to access your citizen page:
citizenship ID; password; Log In

In addition to being able to send messages to other citizens and receive messages from other citizens, from your citizen page you would be able to access the WWW "Community Page". The Community Page would contain links to WWW webpages with announcements about "Travel Exchange", "Homestay Exchange", "Language Exchange", "Culture Exchange", "Work Exchange", and other exchange invitations from WWW citizens to other WWW citizens, as well as links to WWW webpages with announcements about "Tutoring" and "Friendship", et cetera. Following are some examples of announcements that could be posted.

A high school student who lives in Boston and who wants to spend a month of their summer vacation living with the fam-ily of a high school student in France in order to experience and learn about French culture might post an announcement on the Homestay Exchange webpage that says "Boston, France: I am an American high school student who lives in Boston, and I would like to spend a month of my summer vacation living with the fam-ily of a high school student in or near a big city in France. If you are a high school student who lives in or near a big city in France who would like to spend a month of your summer vacation living with me and my family in order to practice your English with me and see Boston and experience living with an American family, please contact me. My citizenship ID is "Boston born and raised, 1998".

A divorced working woman with two young children who lives in New York City and wants to spend a week with her children in Orlando, Florida in the summer to take her children to Walt Disney World and other tourist attractions in Orlando in order to take a break with her kids from New York City in the summer might post an announcement on the Travel Exchange webpage that says "New York City, Orlando: I am a divorced mother of two young children (ages seven and nine) who lives in a two bedroom apartment in New York City (in Brooklyn), and I would like to spend a week in Orlando in the summer in order to be able to take my kids to Walt Disney World and other popular Orlando tourist attractions. If you are a mother with children and live in Orlando, and would like to spend a week in New York City with your children, please contact me so that we can discuss the possibility of you and your children spending a week with me and my children in New York City in exchange for us spending a week with you in Orlando in the summertime. My citizenship ID is "New York mom, Susan and Jason".

A single woman who lives in New Orleans and loves Mardi Gras but would like to experience Carnaval (the Brazilian version of Mardi Gras) in Rio de Janeiro might post an announcement on the Travel Exchange and Culture Exchange webpages that says "Mardi Gras in New Orleans, Carnaval in Rio de Janeiro: I am a single woman who lives in New Orleans and loves Mardi Gras, and I would like to experience the Brazilian version of Mardi Gras in Rio de Janeiro. If you live in Rio de Janeiro and are interested in experiencing the American version of Carnaval (which is called Mardi Gras), please contact me to discuss the possibility of doing a travel and culture exchange in which you spend time with me in New Orleans during Mardi Gras and I spend time with you in Rio de Janeiro during Carnaval. My citizenship ID is "Mardi Gras lover, New Orleans".

A Chinese junior high school student who lives in Beijing and wants to improve his English and experience life in the United States might post an announcement on the Language Exchange,

Culture Exchange, and Homestay Exchange webpages that says "English in America, Chinese in Beijing: I am a Chinese junior high school student who lives with his family in Beijing, and I would like to improve my English and experience life in America by living with the family of an American junior high school student who could help me improve my English. If you are an American junior high school student who is interested in learning Chinese or experiencing life in Beijing, please contact me to discuss the possibility of doing a language exchange, culture exchange, and homestay exchange in which you would experience living with a Chinese family in Beijing and learning some Chinese and I would experience living with an American family in the United States and improving my English. My citizenship ID is "Beijing student, 2003".

An Australian woman who lives and works in Sydney and recently moved into her mother's home because her mother had a stroke and needs constant personal care but cannot afford to pay a person to take care of her mother while she is at work might post an announcement on the Work Exchange webpage that says "Sidney, Australia, personal care help: I am a secretary who lives with her mother in Sydney, Australia, and I need a person who can stay with my mother and take care of her (prepare her meals, feed her, and watch over her) while I am away at work. I am willing to offer room and board (a room with a bed and meals) in exchange for care of my mother while I am away at work during the week, and I can help you practice your English when I am home. You would have free time on the weekends and in the evenings to explore Sydney. Please contact me if you would be interested in helping me with my mother. My citizenship ID is "Sidney secretary, 1985".

An American girl who lost her father in the World Trade Center terrorist attacks in 2001 and who grew up listening to her mother say terrible things about Muslims might post an announcement on the Friendship webpage that says "American girl seeks Muslim friend: I am an American girl who lost her father in the 9/11 terrorist attacks. I have grown up listening to my mother say hateful things about Muslims, but I am tired of hating – I want to replace hate with understanding. I am looking for a Muslim girl interested in making an American friend who can explain to me why some Muslims are moved to kill innocent people through terrorist attacks. Please contact me if you would like to be my friend. My citizenship ID is "American girl, 2001".

A retired Spanish teacher in Colombia who enjoys helping people learn Spanish might post an announcement on the Tutoring webpage that says "Spanish language tutor: I am a retired high school Spanish teacher from Colombia who enjoys helping people learn Spanish and making friends around the world. Please contact me if you would like to communicate with a Spanish language teacher in order to improve your Spanish. My citizenship ID is "Bogota Spanish teacher".

These are just examples of possible announcements that people could post on the WWW community pages. And in order to help convince citizens that other citizens are trustworthy and honest, a "References" section would appear on every citizen page with comments from citizens about a citizen to validate whether that citizen is trustworthy and honest. For example, a reference comment on the citizen page of a person named John might read "I have known John since he began working with me at a bank in 2005. He has always been very responsible, honest, and trustworthy. Please feel free to contact me if you have any questions about John's character. My citizenship ID is...". Reference comments would have to be submitted to the WWW References Department to be approved before being posted on a person's citizen page. This would prevent ex-boyfriends and ex-girlfriends, for example, from posting negative reference comments on a person's citizen page out of anger or spite.

The primary goal of the World Without Walls community would be to bring people together by providing an online meeting place where people from all parts of the world could interact to get to know one another, to learn from one another, and to possibly get together and share experiences together in order to raise the awareness that we are all part of the same global family to move one step closer to creating a heaven on Earth. And what is described here is just the beginning of what could be done with a website designed to create a community to bring the world closer together as a global family.

An Invitation

The video sharing website YouTube was created by three former PayPal employees in February, 2005. In November, 2006, it was bought by Google for 1.65 billion US dollars. The Internet payment company PayPal was established in 1998 and became a wholly owned subsidiary of eBay in 2002. In 2014, PayPal moved $228 billion in 26 currencies across more than 190 nations, generating a total revenue of $7.9 billion. The social networking service Facebook was launched in February, 2004, limiting membership only to Harvard students, but by 2006 allowed anyone above the age of 13 to become a registered user of the website. Its mission is to make the world more open and connected. These three innovations have done a lot to make the world feel more connected. Now imagine what a website designed to teach the world a common language like the My English Childhood website and an online money transfer service like the Internet Payment Network and an online global community like the World Without Walls could do to bring the world together. Could the My English Childhood website and the Internet Payment Network and the World Without Walls have as significant an impact on the world as YouTube, PayPal, and Facebook? There is only one way to find out.

Lacking the information technology knowledge or financial knowledge or business knowledge to make the My English Childhood website and the Internet Payment Network and the

World Without Walls realities by myself, I invite individuals with expertise in any of these areas (and young people who plan to have expertise in any of these areas) who feel enthusiastic about making any one or all three of these innovations a reality to contact me at my primary e-mail address (dleon19@atlanticbb.net) or at my backup e-mail address (dleon1919@yahoo.com). My goal is to attract people interested in working together to make the My English Childhood website and the Internet Payment Network and the World Without Walls realities in order to strengthen communication and community on a global scale and drastically transform our world for the better.

Closing

It is interesting to note that although we have free will, the power to make unconstrained choices, we apparently are not free to choose who we will truly love or what will make us truly happy. When it comes to love, it seems that we can choose who we love and who we do not love, but when it comes to "true love", it does not feel like a matter of choice. Life or destiny or call it whatever you like (Cupid?) appears to decide who we will "fall in love" with, who we will "have chemistry" with. And when it comes to being truly happy, the feeling that we are not in control can be even stronger. Of course, there are levels and varieties of happiness, so I want to differentiate between what I call "ego happiness", which includes "being pleasantly entertained" (like enjoying an entertaining movie) and "being pleasantly distracted" (like doing something to get away from your life, to help you forget whatever pain in your life you are experiencing) and "being pleasantly physically satisfied" (like eating a tasty meal or experiencing some other form of physical gratification), which are popular forms of happiness (of short-lived, fleeting, ego happiness), and what I call "heart happiness", which is rich, deep, profound, fulfilling, impassioned, meaningful happiness that can last a lifetime (and is related to joy, which is felt in the heart, as opposed to pleasure, which is felt in the body). It is that kind of happiness (profound joy: heart happiness) that often feels beyond our power to choose.

Although most of us would like to choose a direction for our lives that conforms with the expectations that our family and others who are important to us have regarding our lives, often we find ourselves feeling that a direction for our lives that does not fit in with the expectations these people have regarding our lives is what might truly make us happy. And that is when it becomes particularly apparent that we are not in control of our lives. Something appears to be guiding our lives by using deep, meaningful happiness like the carrot on a stick is used to guide the direction of a donkey or mule. But do we follow that carrot?

It is reasonable to wonder whether if following that carrot leads to profound happiness, then would not following that carrot lead to unhappiness? Could a majority of people suffering from depression simply be suffering from depression because they choose not to or chose not to follow their carrot? Many people on their death beds suffer from regret, from regretting not having done a particular something or not having tried to pursue a particular path or dream. Imagine getting to the end of your life and feeling regret that you never made an attempt to follow your carrot. Maybe this is why sayings like "follow your bliss" and "be true to yourself" are considered to be so wise. Maybe not following your carrot naturally leads to being unhappy – to not living a fulfilling life.

I find it funny when I hear somebody say that they do not believe in God. I find it funny because I feel God has an effect on our lives whether we believe in God or not, and I say this because we cannot choose what will make us truly happy (heart happy). Something beyond our egos (something I like to call "God") appears to decide that (or appears to have that programmed into our DNA). How many people would you say are profoundly, truly happy? I feel that most people settle for not being unhappy instead of trying to pursue what would make them profoundly, truly, passionately happy, which requires following your carrot, or to put it another way, requires a commitment to growing that unique, special seed that God planted within you. I imagine that most people do not follow that carrot and commit to growing that seed because it may seem too inconceivable and they lack the faith to believe that following that carrot and committing to growing that seed will lead to good things. But what's the alternative? Do you ignore that calling and live within the expectations others have regarding your life and try to be happy with that, and possibly die with regret, or do you follow your bliss and stay true to yourself and have faith that God knows what God is doing with you and live with the consequences? On the one hand, you will live a safe life but risk being unhappy, and on the other hand, you can follow your carrot and commit to growing your seed and see where it takes you.

That's a decision we all have to make. Maybe following your carrot and committing to growing your seed will lead to seeming failure (like it did for Jesus Christ and Gandhi and Abraham Lincoln and Martin Luther King, who all died – who were all killed – for following their carrot) but at least your life will have purpose and feel meaningful, and at least you will die with the conviction of knowing that your life was not just about yourself (about your ego needs), but rather, about something much greater than yourself that felt bigger than life, and death. You have to decide what you want to live for, what you are willing to die for, and what you will eventually trade your life for. And not making a decision about that is also a decision.

No one really knows why they are alive
until they know what they'd die for.
– Martin Luther King

The two most important days in your life are
the day you are born and the day you find out why.
– Mark Twain

Made in the USA
Columbia, SC
03 September 2018